Wi gibit theingks langa Dedi God blanga dijan stori blanga Jeims en Anjelina ministri. Longtaim CMA bin irrim det trabul bin hepin langa Ropa Riba. Deibin jandim siksbala mishanri olabat blanga seibumbat, lenimbat en dalimbat olabat det Gudnynus. If detlot mishanri mob nomo bina kaman, wal melabat nomo bina jidan laibala tudei. Im brabli sedwan stori dijan. Nomeda dubala bin abum adtaim, bat dubala bin trastimbat Jisas olawei. Burrum 1908 melabat tjetj en det ministri bin kipgon jidan strongbalawei raidap tudei. Wi gudbinji na.

We thank God for James and Angelina's ministry. When CMA heard of the trouble at Roper River, they sent those six missionaries to protect, teach and bring the good news. If they had not come, we would not be alive today. Their sufferings sadden us, but they kept on following Jesus. So we are encouraged. Since 1908, our church and ministries have continued strongly, with Aboriginal leaders who followed their example.

Rev William Hall and **Rev Marjorie Hall**, deacons at St Matthew's Church, Ngukurr

James and Angelina's story of faith, sacrifice and mission continues to inspire Indigenous and non-Indigenous Christians alike.

I commend the author's desire to see their legacy live on and pray that this account will encourage many to follow Jesus faithfully, just as James and Angelina did.

Rev Neville Naden,
Indigenous Ministry Officer,
The Bush Church Aid Society

When I lived at Ngukurr, people told me that it was James Noble who brought them the gospel. The combination of Angelina and James' unique gifts resulted in a positive contribution to mission. Their story deserves a wider audience.

Rev Dr Joy Sandefur,
spent 25 years working in the Northern Territory with Wycliffe Bible Translators and The Bush Church Aid Society

Dr Kuan's compact account of James and Angelina Noble's ministry is a story that we need to hear clearly. Aboriginal people can genuinely become Christians, and their own gospel-witness in word and action can bring great blessing to other Aboriginal people and the wider nation. An important dimension to their effectiveness is the strategic benefit of language-learning, in which Angelina excelled. Read this book!

Rt Rev Dr Greg Anderson,
Anglican Bishop of the Northern Territory

James and Angelina Noble were devoted Christian people, proudly Aboriginal and significant Australians. Their loyal, self-effacing and lifelong contribution to the future of their own people and to Christian mission should never be forgotten. In this well-researched and sensitively written publication, Wei-Han Kuan has brought Angelina and James back to life.

Rev Dr John Harris,
author of *One Blood*

White missionaries brought the gospel to James and Angelina Noble and infused in them a commitment to a missionary faith that ended up serving First Peoples across Queensland, the Northern Territory and North West Australia. I strongly recommend this book to all who are interested in Christian mission to and by First Australians.

Tanya Costello,
Vice President of the
Church Missionary Society Australia

For many years, mission history has focused on well-known heroes. More recently, historians have been recovering the stories of those who served from positions that did not carry power or privilege. I am delighted that Dr Kuan is restoring the voice of James and Angelina Noble. Their contribution to mission deserves to be widely known.

Rev Dr David Williams,
Principal of St Andrew's Hall,
Federal Training College of the
Church Missionary Society Australia

I Speak for Black People
The story of pioneer Christian missionaries James and Angelina Noble

Wei-Han Kuan

broad continent

First published in 2025
Broad Continent Publishing
PO Box 198, Forest Hill Victoria 3131, Australia
management@broadcontinent.com.au
www.broadcontinent.com.au

Hardcover: ISBN 978-0-6484234-3-0
Paperback: ISBN 978-0-6484234-2-3

A catalogue record for this work is available
from the National Library of Australia.

Wei-Han Kuan is the Executive Director of the Church Missionary Society Victoria. His doctoral research in Anglican evangelical history focused on the themes of leadership and long-term continuity. It has been published as *Foundations of Anglican Evangelicalism in Victoria, 1847–1937*. With his wife and three children, Wei-Han is a part of St Alfred's Anglican Church, Blackburn North.

AUSTRALIA

Scale of English Miles

50   0   100   200   300

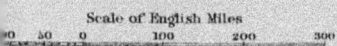

Railways thus

C. Bougainville   C. Londonderry

Bathurst I.   Victoria
Clarence Str. Adam B.
Port Darwin
Port Patterson   Anson B.
C. Blaze   Southport
C. Hotham   B. Pearce

Admiralty Gulf
Montague S.
Bigge I.   Queens Channel
York Sd.
Roe R.   Cambridge Gulf
Prince Regent   Glenelg   Wyndham
Brunswick B.
Vulcan Pt.
Collier B.   Mt. Cockburn
Buccaneer Arch.   District
Sunday I.
C. Lévèque   KIMBERLEY
Beagle B.   King
C. Baskerville   Leopold Ra.
Ord R.   DIVISION
C. Boileau   Dampier   Land
Broome   Sound   Fitzroy R.
Roebuck Bay   Hall's Creek
Lagrange B.   Latouche Treville   Fitzroy R.   Mt. Barrett
Boasut   Margaret   NOR
Rich grassy country   Sturt Cr.
Mt. Bannerman   Sandy Desert

DIAN
Mardi Hills   A. C. Gregory
Amphinome   Sandy   Godfreys   Salt Lakes
OCEAN   Shoals   Joanna Spr.   Tank   A. C. Gregory   Stuart May
Condon
Dampier   L. Isabella   A. C. Gregory   Fisher Cr.
Arch.   TER
Roeburne   WEST   DIV   Great Sandy Desert
L. White 1879
Onslow   L. T. Gregory   Helena Spr.
YORK   Shaw R.   Salt Marsh   Mt. Fr
Hammersley Rh.   Family W. 1896-7
Hooley   Mt. Samson   Rich grassy country   Tropic of Capricorn
Warton Hills   Carnegie 1896-7   Mt. D
Waterloo R.   WESTERN   Giles 1876   L. Macdonald
Mt. Augustus   Giles 1876   Amadeus   Mt. Olga
Mt. Labouchere   Alfred &   Petermann Ra.
Marie Ra.   L. Christopher   Ayer's
Gascoyne R.   Wild Spr.   Forrest 1874   Mt. Charles
CO N   Windich Spr.   Sutherland   Mussa
Murchison R.   L. Augusta   Ra.   Range
Mt. Murchison   Alexander Spr.   Mt. Worsnop
Nannine   L. Wells   Empress Spr.   Mt. Flemming
AUSTRALIA   EASTERN   DIVISION
Cue   Elder 1892
L. Austin   L. Darlot
E. Mt. Magnet   L. Sir Thomas Elder
Salt Marshes   Baron v Muller   Elder 1892
Victoria Ra.   L. Carey
Boundary   Dam
Great Victoria Desert   Salt Lakes   SOUT
L. Barlee   Giles 1875
L. Monger   Menzies   Youldeh
Herschel   Ularing   Queen Victoria Spr.   Eucla
Mt. Churchman   Kalgoorlie   Salt Lakes   Kubra   Head of the Gre
Australian Bight
Mt. Kennel   Coolgardie   C. Adieu
L. Brown   Mt. Robinson
New Norcia   L. Lefroy   Great
Breton R.   L. Cowan   Australian
Moore R.   Bova Yidin   Charlina L.   Davert   Bight
Perth   Boyadyn   Dundas H.   Eyre 1840   Mt. Giver
York
Canning   Bremar Ra.
Toodyay   Salt Lakes
Williamsburgh   Russell R.   Israelite B.
Katanning   Esperance   Arid
Boullia I.   Mondrain L.
Stirling Ra.   Recherche Arch.
Leeuwin   King George Sound
C. Chatham   Peak Head
C. Entrecasteaux

INDIAN   OCEAN

Gulf of Carpentaria
Cape York Peninsula
CORAL SEA
Great Barrier
QUEENSLAND
NEW SOUTH WALES
VICTORIA
AUSTRALIA
TORY
English Company Is.
Melville B.
C. Arnhem
Caledon B.
Blue Mud B.
Groote Eylandt
Limmen Bight
Limmen B. R.
Sir Edward Pellew Group
Wellesley Is.
Mornington I.
Bentinck I.
Burketown
Normanton
Croydon
Shelburne B.
C. Grenville
Temple B.
Weymouth B.
Lloyd B.
C. Direction
C. Sidmouth
Princess Charlotte B.
Flinders I.
C. Melville
Howick Is.
Lizard I.
C. Flattery
C. Bedford
Cooktown
Maytown
Bloomfield R.
C. Tribulation
Trinity Bay
Palmerville
P. Douglas
Cairns
C. Grafton
Herberton
Bellenden Ker Hills
Rockingham B.
Hinchinbrook I.
Palm Is.
Halifax B.
Cardwell
Townsville
Bowling Green B.
Wickham
Cumberland
C. Hillsborough
Mackay
Holmes Rf.
Mitchell R.
Gilbert R.
Gilberton
Charters Towers
Hughenden
Flinders R.
Richmond
Cloncurry
Barclay Downs
Boulia
Winton
Collingwood
Muttaburra
Bowen Downs
Aramac
Clermont
Barcaldine
Isisford
Blackall
Tambo
Springsure
Charleville
Adavale
Roma
Mitchell
Toowoomba
Warwick
Cunnamulla
Bollon
Nocundra
Hungerford
Bourke
Cobar
Wilcannia
Broken Hill
Menindie
Wentworth
Balranald
Hay
Deniliquin
Bathurst
Wellington
Dubbo
Goulburn
Tamworth
Newcastle
Sydney
Wollongong
Kiama
Shoalhaven R.
Jervis B.
Ulladulla
Bateman B.
Mt. Kosciusko 7310
Townsend 7350
Melbourne
Bendigo
Ballarat
Darling R.
Murray R.
Lachlan R.
Murrumbidgee
Cooper's Cr.
Great Stony Desert
Grey Range
Barrier Range
Mt. Hopeless
L. Eyre
L. Frome
L. Torrens
L. Gairdner
Port Augusta
Hawker
Adelaide
Spencer G.
Investigator Str.
Kangaroo I.
Encounter Bay
C. Jaffa
C. Northumberland
Eyres Peninsula
Gawler Ranges
Flinders Ra.
Killpatha
Coast Ra.
Amazon Lag.
Mt. Playford
Marshall R.
L. Caroline
Hay R.
Todd R.

Foreword

Angelina and James Noble deserve to be better known by Australian Christians. I am so pleased that this volume is being published in time to celebrate the centenary of James' ordination as the first Aboriginal Anglican clergyman in Australia. However, as this story makes clear, theirs was a partnership in missionary ministry that would not have been possible without Angelina's exceptional gifts and abilities. It is so good to see a clearer account of her great contribution to the church.

I first heard of the Nobles while living in North Queensland, where they were born and experienced the early part of their Christian formation and ministry. Much of their formation took place at Yarrabah, a place from which many significant Aboriginal Christian leaders have emerged. I am grateful that this volume expands on what I have written previously about their lives there as well as their important contribution to the Mitchell River mission.

Our Aboriginal and Indigenous brothers and sisters have long understood that mission is part of their response to the grace of God in Christ. After all, deep in their memory is the knowledge that missionaries brought them the gospel to begin with, and hence they too had a responsibility to take the gospel to others in their communities and further afield. This is exactly what I saw a whole generation of Aboriginal leaders doing when I was Bishop of the Northern Territory. In this, they were following the example of James and Angelina Noble, and it was my joy to encourage and facilitate their endeavours as much as possible.

My prayer is that the Angelina and James Noble story will grow as a source of inspiration and encouragement for the Australian Aboriginal, Indigenous and Torres Strait Islander church—and for Christians everywhere pursuing the mission of God to bring his whole word to his whole world.

+Philip
Bishop of the Northern Territory 1999–2006
Archbishop of Melbourne 2006–2025

Contents

Myall man at the Forrest River Mission.
1925

I am very lone. I am the only black people left. When I speak like this you know what I mean. I wish we could come back two or three hundred years ago, and there were plenty of blacks, and we might have saved them, but it is now too late.
It is not your fault; but they tried to live like you, so they died. The only way to save their life is Christian grace and teaching.

Alone they will die out because they have no country of their own. They have no black people to stand and speak for them when I die. I can speak for those black people …

James Noble,
addressing the Ninth Australian
Church Congress, Melbourne, May 1925

That September, James Noble became the first Aboriginal Australian to be admitted to Holy Orders in the Anglican Church. He was ordained deacon in St George's Cathedral Perth and the event made news across the country.

Through the preceding months James Noble had accompanied his mentor Ernest Gribble on a tour around Australia, telling the story of their missions and the great needs as well as advances made in assisting black people in their country. In Melbourne, James was received on the platform with a standing tribute from all present—bishops, other presenters, the entire large audience. He was "the Aboriginal with the spiritual face."[1]

A few years later, their hard-won gains were dealt a fatal blow. James was called on to serve as a tracker to investigate one of the last large-scale massacres of Australian Aboriginal people by whites. We will never know exactly how many men, women and children perished—certainly scores, perhaps many more. Justice simply took too long to serve. The local white community turned against the Forrest River Mission. Gribble, and eventually the Nobles, left.

James and Angelina's story features in every major history of Aboriginal Christianity and deserves to be better known by all Australians. Most of this material first appeared in a *Festschrift* for Philip Freier, whose own doctoral dissertation on the history of the Mitchell River Mission, Kowanyama, introduces us to Angelina's story.[2] James Noble has an entry in the Australian Dictionary of Biography;[3] and a small self-published booklet by Geoff Higgins contains much early material,[4] but nothing more substantive has been published until now that also includes Angelina's important story.

A century on, what lessons are there to be learnt from the story of James and Angelina Noble? How might their lives and experiences instruct and inspire us? What lessons might be drawn from their steadfast faith in the face of much suffering and opposition? Does James still declare, from across the ages, "I speak for black people"?

The Rev James Noble was
a pioneer missionary
and the first Indigenous
Australian to be ordained
in the Anglican Church.

1933

Early years

James Noble is most commonly introduced as Australia's first ordained Aboriginal minister, deaconed at St George's Anglican Cathedral, Perth on 13 September 1925.[5] A photograph of him confirms the many descriptions of him as a striking man: six feet tall, athletic, handsome, with an intelligent and indeed noble bearing.[6]

James was born in 1876 near Normanton in the western gulf country of North Queensland.[7] As a teenager he began working as a drover, moving cattle stock between the Doyle family properties of Riversleigh on the Gregory River in Queensland and Invermien near Scone in New South Wales. Alec Doyle recounted his memory of Noble asking his father, James Doyle, to be allowed to stay at Invermien and be educated.[8] The elder James agreed, and Noble was taken under the family's wing. He was given employment during the day, and James Doyle organised for him to be educated by staff from the nearby Scone Grammar School.

James' intelligence and sense of humour is apparent in this Alec Doyle recollection:

> During a visit to Scone, Bishop [Stanton] stayed at Invermien, and went for a walk in the garden before breakfast. Seeing a black boy raking the garden path he went over to have a word with him, and, to open the conversation, said, "That fella Mr Doyle: how long he bin sit down alonga Invermien?" He was somewhat shattered by Noble's reply, "My Lord, Mr Doyle has resided at Invermien for the past thirteen years."[9]

The Doyles were observant Christians and together with the Doyle children Noble attended Sunday school classes at St Luke's Scone. The name James Noble is entered into the parish's baptismal register on 1 July 1895. This is the earliest written record of his Christian name. Was he named after his patron James Doyle?

Formal baptismal records only tell part of the story. Here is James' own account of his conversion:

> Before I became a Christian … I was a bush native. My mother and father died in the bush. I first saw white people when I went to a station in the Leichardt country and at that time I was only a boy. I stayed there for a long time and the station owner took me to his home at Scone, N.S.W. All that time I had been droving. I learned to read at the

Grammar School at Scone. I reached the fourth class at school, and up to that time I had heard a lot about prayers, religion and churches. Then a missionary came along and lectured on missions ... He was the Rev. Mr. Boyce. That was when I heard the real things that influenced me. I felt I wanted to do some good. I wanted to go to New Guinea, where Mr. Boyce came from, but I was not permitted to do that, owing to the prevalence, of disease there.

I was at Townsville for three or four years and afterwards at Yarrabah, where Mr. Gribble was stationed, and I stayed there with him. I was not a missionary at that time, but was wishing that some day I would be.[10]

In recalling his conversion, what stood out for Noble were the missionary origins and missionary impulse of his Christian faith.[11]

Within a few seasons, the much cooler climate of New South Wales began to have a deleterious effect on the young Noble's health. He was sent to live with Canon Alfred Edwards, Rector of Hughenden, in North Queensland. Edwards had studied at Moore College and been ordained in Sydney for the Diocese of North Queensland in 1880. He had been immediately posted as a missionary to Herbert River. He was honoured for his service in the north when he was appointed an honorary canon of North Queensland in 1887. It seems that he was selected as just the right kind of mentor for the young mission-minded man.[12] Unfortunately, Edwards died on 12 February 1898, not long after Noble's arrival.

This was a potentially disastrous development for Noble. His athletic prowess attracted the attention of racing promoters who saw a money-making opportunity. This account was recorded later:

> Mr. Gribble told of an early experience in the career of his dusky friend when he was asked to fall victim to the wiles of well known sporting celebrities who were profoundly impressed by his ability on the running track … However "James" was not persuaded to discard his mission ambitions.
>
> When the interviewer ventured the suggestion that he must have been very smart on the track to attract so much notice, "James," who was standing close at hand popped his head around the door and smilingly acknowledged that that was so. "One hundred and fifty yards in fourteen seconds," he admitted.[13]

That is fast by any standard. At this time, Christopher Barlow, Bishop of North Queensland, "took considerable interest in Noble."[14] Barlow's churchmanship has been described as initially evangelical but moving to a more moderate liberalism with a focus on spirituality in worship and personal faith of the clergy.[15] These were James' earlier years, and Barlow considered Noble in danger of drifting, so he asked the missionary at Yarrabah to take him on. Thus James Noble arrived at Yarrabah some time in 1898.[16] It was there that James Noble began his long association with Christian ministry, mission work, and his mentor Ernest Gribble. It was also at Yarrabah that James Noble met his future wife, Angelina.

Angelina Noble's early history ought to fill the contemporary Australian reader's heart with great sadness, anger and a steely determination to confront the wrongs of our past. She was born in an Aboriginal community near Winton, Queensland, around 1879 but kidnapped as a young girl by a white man, a travelling horse trader.[17] She was, in outback slang, a "stockman's boy": an Aboriginal girl with hair cut short and dressed as boy, forced to accompany the man through his travels and function as his concubine. Renamed "Tommy," her sexual slavery came to an end when the local police around Cairns freed her. She was immediately sent to the mission at Yarrabah. Higgins records the memory of Ernestine Yeatman, "an old Yarrabah identity":

She [Angelina] came over here in a stockman's suit, cowboy hat and everything; riding boots. When the police brought her down from the

The Roper River Mission was founded
by Mr Reg Joynt, Rev George Huthnance
and Mr Charles Sharpe from Victoria,
and James Noble, Horace Reid and
Angelina Noble from Queensland.
1908

jailhouse in Cairns they thought she was a young man. She never showed that she was a girl till they found out when they were doing their toilet, you know. They found she was a woman. They got a surprise.[18]

Yeatman also reported that, "Angelina was very young when she married James Noble." A photograph of the couple with Horace Reid reproduced by Higgins seems to confirm that assessment.[19]

James Noble's first wife had been Margaret "Maggie" Frew. They were married by 1900.[20] When compared to the written records, the chronology and details of the next two years seem to have been confused in the memories collected by Higgins; details subsequently followed by later writers.[21] The trauma of these early years could have easily confused the memory of secondhand witnesses as they recollected to Higgins some seventy years later.

James and Maggie had a daughter, Blanche Margaret, who only lived ten months from July 1901 to May 1902.[22] Maggie was described as "a nice gentle girl, but very delicate," and she died in April 1902, a month before her child's death.

Not long after, James and Lizzie Moore, the first matron of the Yarrabah hospital, were engaged. Sadly, Lizzie died just before the set wedding date in July 1902.[23] She had contracted a fatal disease from one of her patients.

James and Angelina Noble were married on 15 October 1902.[24] A son, James Hilton, was born on 17 August 1903 but died later that year.

The few years between 1898 and 1903 were clearly tumultuous ones for James and Angelina. On his side there had been ill-health, a move from New South Wales to Queensland, possible spiritual wandering, the death of a mentor he barely got to know, a new life at Yarrabah, and the deaths of a wife, a fiancée and two children. On her side there had been a torrid experience of kidnapping, slavery and abuse, ended by her rescue and arrival at Yarrabah in early 1902. She was baptised on 25 July 1902, married less than two months after, then soon pregnant, giving birth but losing James Hilton after only a few months.

James and Angelina were therefore both no strangers to suffering. Suffering however did not embitter them. Christian faith transformed their experience of suffering into enduring missionary service in the name of Jesus Christ.

Angelina, James and their
two daughters on the eve
of their departure for the
Forrest River Mission.
1914

Rev James Noble conducts a christening
at the Forrest River Mission.

1925

Yarrabah Mission

The Yarrabah Bellenden Kerr Mission had been founded by Rev John Gribble outside Cairns in 1892, only six years before James Noble's arrival.[25] Gribble was a missionary and fierce advocate for Aboriginal peoples. He dared to take on the colonial establishment of the day, and paid a high personal price for it.[26] In John Harris' assessment, John Gribble was driven by his sense of the absolute necessity of personal salvation found in Christ, his outrage at the injustices against Aboriginal people, and the failure of the Christian community to bring them the knowledge of Jesus Christ. Yarrabah was the last in a line of missions founded by Gribble as a place of refuge, protection and instruction, but he died in 1893 before the mission could be fully established. That work was left to his son Ernest Gribble.

Ernest Gribble took up his father's work and travelled extensively through the region to encourage people to come to Yarrabah to receive refuge, medical help and training in practical skills. Harris describes how Gribble found very many children in the surrounding fringe camps, "orphaned, starving and diseased," very young addicts of opium and alcohol, and very young girls having been abused by Europeans, and Chinese and Filipino traders. In Harris' view, it was Gribble's passion to rescue these children that led to rapid early growth at Yarrabah.[27]

Gribble's philosophy was to "place as much trust as possible in the most able of the people."[28] He delighted to list the roles occupied by Aboriginal people at Yarrabah: organists, music teachers, dispensary matron, motor mechanic, engineer in charge of the mission's launch boat, an ex-prisoner now drummer in the brass band, a dentist extracting and filling teeth, sacristan and server at the church, and printers at the mission press.

Aboriginal people had leading roles in the Yarrabah hospital and on several farms growing vegetables, fruit, cotton, dairy cows and pigs. The mission also had an operating fire brigade that carried out weekly training and a rifle corps. It was not all work and no fun: there were also a sailing club, sports teams, and a subsequently famous brass band.[29] Yarrabah's Court of Justice met weekly to deal with "complaints and misbehaviour." Menmuny, or King John, an early convert and recognised elder, played a leading role as its president. In spiritual matters, Aboriginal men like Alick Bybee were free to take the initiative to organise and preach at informal services for Aborigines camped on the fringes of the mission compound.[30]

By the time James and Angelina Noble were married at Yarrabah in 1902 it had become home to perhaps a hundred people and was a place of life and industry, worship and social progress. James moved quickly into leadership and was noted as an able preacher and teacher of the faith. He held a lay reader's licence and was Yarrabah's representative to the North Queensland Synod. In 1905, there were no less than nine outstations. The largest of these at Bukki Creek was under James' direction with Angelina playing a vital role alongside. Their early years of marriage at Yarrabah were years of training and development for what was to come.

Angelina and James Noble and Roper River
children with the lugger *Francis Pritt*.
The tallest boy is James Japanma who later
became a noted evangelist.
1908

The Mitchell River expedition

James and Angelina's potential for missionary work was recognised as early as 1904, when they were selected to accompany Gribble to Mitchell River on the western side of North Queensland to explore starting a similar work there. It was probably at this point that James Noble first considered himself "a missionary" in fulfilment of his early ambitions.

A mission at Mitchell River had been envisaged for some time by the Bishop of Carpentaria, Gilbert White.[31] In 1904, a full-scale missionary expedition involving Gribble and three white and six Yarrabah Aboriginal missionaries, including the Nobles, was undertaken.

The presence of the Aboriginal men certainly assisted but Angelina's contribution was perhaps the more significant for building trust among the locals. Philip Freier writes of her contribution to the expedition:

> The presence of Angelina Noble had opened
> up for the missionaries a whole new domain
> of interaction and confidence with the
> women and children. Whilst bush Aborigines

had seen Aboriginal men as native police, stockmen or general retainers to whites, it is most unlikely that they would have encountered an Aboriginal woman travelling freely with her husband in a party of whites. The main experience of Aboriginal women with whites was that of rape or abduction into concubinage, with those Aboriginal women on the station precincts mostly detained against their will. Coming as she had through these experiences herself, Angelina would have been well placed to understand the apprehensions of the Aboriginal women and their fears for the safety of their own children in the presence of whites.[32]

Angelina's gender and linguistic and relational gifts were the keys to her ability to win trust from the locals. Angelina was able to learn the story of one of the bush women who, curiously, was able to speak English: how she had been abducted, lived among the whites where she had learnt the language, and then escaped to return to her tribe with a child who had been fathered by a white man.[33]

The party returned to Yarrabah, having laid the foundations for a new mission later known as Kowanyama.

Roper River Mission

Four years later, James and Angelina Noble's missionary focus and desire led to them volunteering to join three white missionaries from the Victorian Church Missionary Association on a founding expedition to the Roper River in East Arnhem Land in the Northern Territory.[34] The CMA was a progenitor of the present-day Church Missionary Society. It had overseen the Aboriginal work at Lake Condah and Lake Tyers in Victoria since the mid-1800s. In 1906, news reached south of the injustices and desperate situation for Aboriginal people in Arnhem Land. Pastoral lease holders, most notably the massive London-based Eastern and African Cold Storage Company, were determined to clear their land. The Company employed gangs of men to hunt and shoot on sight all Aboriginal inhabitants.[35]

Despite being in a parlous financial state, the Victorian CMA determined that God was calling them north. The collective determination of that generation of Christians is still stirring reading today.[36] An exploratory visit to Roper River was made by Bishop Gilbert White and the CMA's General Secretary

Dressed for a circumcision ceremony at
Roper River. Christian leaders continued
this cultural practice well into the 1960s.
1908

Rev Arthur Ebbs in 1907. The necessary funds were raised by 1908, and George Huthnance, Reg Joynt and Charles Sharpe were sent. Practical as well as spiritual qualifications were needed. Huthnance, a farmer and teacher, was ordained specifically for the role, Joynt was a teacher, and Sharp a stockman.[37]

They visited the successful mission at Yarrabah en route and, close to the end of their fortnight's stay, called for volunteers to join them. James and Angelina Noble and Horace Reid stepped forward. Horace was reputedly Yarrabah's best builder and had obtained the highest marks in the Queensland Anglican Church's Sunday school examinations.[38] The group's leader, Huthnance, was initially reluctant to take a woman on the hazardous and demanding enterprise. A secret community ballot was held, and the unanimous verdict was that the highly valued and accomplished Angelina should go. One boy apparently wrote, "Please send Angelina because she can do work among the women men could not do."[39] He was absolutely right.

Higgins extracted this report of the event from the Yarrabah newspaper, dated 21 August 1908:

All Yarrabah is much stirred at the going of James, Angelina, and Horace to the Roper River Mission. Their loss is a great one to our mission, but the satisfaction that we are really helping on another mission to the

The first Christian service at
the Roper River Mission.
1908

Aborigines more than makes up for the loss.

James and Angelina are a splendid couple, and the sorrow at their going was very sincere, especially at Bukki Creek where James had long been lay reader …

We had some grand services before they left. On the Wednesday night … we had a dismissal service. Dadda (Gribble) spoke to us about home at Yarrabah; and asked them to never forget it, but to come back when they had done their duty … but if God did not wish them to return to their home at Yarrabah, then there was still another and better home where we might be reunited when we have done our work for God …

James spoke for a little while, saying he would like to say a lot, but could not. He spoke of his love for Yarrabah and the longing that some of them had to help many more of their brothers and sisters. He knew that God had called him to leave his beautiful home—the happiest life he had ever had—to go and help those blacks who were wild, wild as he himself had been for many years. He would never forget us, but go away to obey our Lord Jesus Christ who had left his own most beautiful home to come and help us live on earth …

We were all sorry to part, but neither we
nor they would have had them turn back.
We love them too well for that. They will
earn a brighter crown because they have
taken up the cross of self denial to follow our
dear Saviour, Jesus Christ. We cannot help
feeling proud at Yarrabah.[40]

James Noble was at last realising the missionary
ambitions first sown in him at his conversion. The
Yarrabah missionaries' perspective was eternal,
knowing that they might never return home, but an
eternal lodging and reunification with loved ones in
Christ awaited them. They looked to the Lord Jesus
as their exemplar: just at Christ had left his beautiful
home to serve them, they would leave their home to
serve their "wild" black brothers and sisters.

The work at Roper River got off to a flying start
as the local Aborigines realised that the mission was
a place of refuge and safety. White and Ebbs' previous visits, and the presence of the three black Yarrabah missionaries—including a woman—accelerated
acceptance and trust. Gajiyuma, a respected elder
who had met White and Ebbs earlier, led the way in
gathering people from various clans at Roper River
for refuge. Harris records the words of Barnabas
Roberts, an Alawa man, who was a young boy at
the time: "If the missionaries hadn't come, my tribe
would have been all shot down."[41]

Refuge was an important motivator and theme. However, equally as significant was the coming of the gospel. Gajiyuma died in peace at Roper River within a year of the mission's founding with these final words in Kriol on his lips, recorded by Rex Joynt, "Jesus bin talking alonga me. Him bin tell me no more be frightened to die. Me no more frightened fella."[42]

For reasons of persistent ill-health the Nobles were to depart and return to Yarrabah by June 1910— serving less than two full years at Roper River. That same year Horace Reid moved to Katherine. Despite the relative brevity of their time there, the Yarrabah missionaries were remembered for years and generations afterwards as the ones who brought the gospel to Ngukurr, as the Roper River community is now known. James Noble exercised a preaching and teaching ministry of a kind that meant that his name in particular was associated with the coming of the gospel.[43]

The interior of the church at
the Forrest River Mission.
1925

Forrest River Mission

By 1908 Ernest Gribble had served at Yarrabah for eighteen years. He was exhausted and suffered a breakdown. Hospitalised in Brisbane, he never fully recovered and resigned in May 1910 to become Rector of Gosford, New South Wales. Neither he nor his friends the Nobles ever gave up their missionary spirit and identity. Upon his return to Yarrabah James Noble wrote to Gribble asking that if he were ever to start another mission, "to send for him at once."[44]

James did not have to wait long. In 1913 an urgent plea for help came from the Bishop of North West Australia, Gerald Trower. The Forrest River Mission in the Kimberley was in danger of collapse. Just as at Roper River, pastoralists were clearing the land of Aboriginal people. However, at Forrest River, the Aboriginal inhabitants were more willing to counter violence with violence. Trower recognised the danger and reached out to the day's pre-eminent missionary to the Aborigines who had made such a success of Yarrabah. Gribble was quick to take on the new challenge, and just as quick to enlist the help of his trusted friends and capable missionaries, James and Angelina Noble. They arrived from Yarrabah in April 1914.

Gribble wrote to the Secretary of the Australian Board of Mission (ABM) calling for one other missionary. The *ABM Review* of June 1914 called for that volunteer and carried this statement with regard to the conditions of service at its Forrest River Mission:

> The Mission has for its object the conversion to Christianity of the Aborigines of the North West, and their advancement in civilisation by means of education and by instructing them in such kinds of work as are suited to the climate of their country ...
>
> The Bishop is unable to offer any inducement in the way of salary. It is necessary that those who join the Mission should do so with the single desire to live for, and willingness, if it be so, to die in their work because it is Christ's.[45]

The risks were real, and conditions typically difficult. Gribble arrived and acted in his typical authoritarian style but, unlike the previous missionaries, showed real kindness in tending to the sick and injured rather than constructing walls and putting up barbed wire around the camp. Importantly, just as at Yarrabah, Gribble was willing to empower the locals.

Once the Nobles arrived, the team began to accelerate their work of giving practical as well as spiritual instruction. Within the first year, a large number attended weekly services, where James led and preached regularly. A school was opened, and locals learnt to trust their children to the mission school, leaving them there for lessons when the rest of their context was unsafe for children.

Angelina played a key part in this, as a black woman with children there whom the local women could trust. Three children were born to the Nobles at Forrest River. Angelina's linguistic gifts were also critical—especially as James was weak in this area. According to the Nobles' daughter, Love Kiuna, who was born at Forrest River, her father never really picked up the local language and was limited to his native language from Normanton. By contrast, Angelina spoke "five languages over there" as well as "the language from Darwin."[46] Angelina translated for James, Gribble and public authorities. Her linguistic capacity would have been matched by the cultural insight that comes from learning a new tongue. She was the only woman worker at Forrest River for at least six years, in charge of the school dormitory, health care, doing all the baking, and teaching cooking and laundry skills.[47] It was no wonder at all that Gribble had the highest esteem for her as a missionary.[48]

Angelina and James Noble's house
at the Forrest River Mission.
1925

Progress in the first eleven years was rapid, with many conversions and baptisms. James Noble declared:

> Too often I hear people say you can't teach the black man. When I hear a man say that, I ask, "Well what am I?" God is strong, and the missionary does good things in His name. Eleven years ago they were all heathen people at Forrest River. Then Mr. Gribble came and devoted his life to the Master. He came to try and save the black people, and God has blessed his work. Instead of the wild bush and nothing else at Forrest River, there is now a cross standing.
>
> Once upon a time black people ate black people. All people like meat, and black people like it, too, but Mr. Gribble came and the good news spread. "No more cannibalism." They put all that away. God is strong.[49]

In early 1925, Gribble and James Noble embarked on what would become a successful nine-month missionary deputation tour throughout Australia, telling the story of the Forrest River Mission and calling for more support. The tour began in Perth, and included Kalgoorlie, Collie, Bunbury, Adelaide, Port Pirie, Melbourne, Geelong, Sydney, Newcastle, and Brisbane.[50]

The Forrest River Mission. Two hundred children attended Angelina's school. The community's stock included 1500 cattle, 1000 horses and donkeys, and 500 sheep.

1925

The Missionary Exhibition in Bedford Hall, Perth illustrates the typical format. It was opened by the Archbishop on the Tuesday evening on 10 March 1925 and ran for three days. Curios from China, New Guinea and Forrest River were on show and on sale. James Noble spoke three times each day.[51] As the tour progressed, it became apparent that James' heartfelt and impassioned presentations were a powerful drawcard. In Adelaide, James had such an effect on the locals that a social gathering was organised in his honour. The *Glenelg Guardian* reported that:

> Mr. James Noble, the aboriginal preacher
> ... has won the hearts of everyone and has
> made many friends during the time he has
> been in the parish. The social committee
> felt that they could not let him leave for his
> home without showing him in some way
> their feelings of love and respect. Quite a
> large number of parishioners were present
> at the Kiosk Hall on Friday night, and
> Mr. Noble was given a rousing reception.[52]

In Newcastle it was reported that "Mr. James Noble, who has become exceedingly popular among the exhibition audiences, spoke in an earnest, sincere way on the good effects upon those of his countrymen in the passing from Heathenism to Christianity."[53]

It was also in Newcastle that Gribble reported on having more than two hundred children in the mission school, 1500 cattle, 1000 horses and donkeys, 500 sheep and other stock. James had the opportunity to publicly acknowledge and give credit to Angelina. He declared that much of the success of the mission was due to Angelina and her facility with languages—having learnt the local Forrest River language within the first six months, and subsequently also gaining the other languages used locally. James also revealed that he hoped to one day visit England, however he declared in his next breath, "My creed is a simple one, I go where I can preach."[54]

Higgins reports that in Melbourne, as James came onto the platform before a large gathering, the entire audience including the bishops and other speakers on the platform rose "as one man in homage ... to the Aboriginal with the spiritual face."[55]

The tour culminated in James Noble's ordination as a deacon at St George's Cathedral, Perth that September.[56] He had been studying for ordination for a number of months, possibly encouraged by Bishop Trower, almost certainly by the ABM and Gribble. Reporting on the ordination, the *ABM Review* printed the following:

> James Noble's life has been one of Christian service for the benefit of his race, and the

steps taken in ordaining him was [*sic*] not hastily taken. In every way he has proved himself worthy of the office to which he has now been appointed in the church, and will, we hope, be the first of a long line of native clergy as in other churches in ancient and modern times.[57]

It seemed that James and Angelina's missionary work at Forrest River was poised for fresh growth and new possibilities. But it was not to be. Their sufferings were not yet complete.

Rev Ernest Gribble and Ronald from the Forrest River Mission search through ashes for charred bones at the site of a massacre.

1926

Forrest River massacres

In July 1922 a group of police on the hunt for cattle killers had entered the Marndoc Aboriginal Reserve in which the mission was located, and massacred a large number of Aborigines. Locals reported to Gribble that "the country all stink from the dead fellows." The safety of the reserve had been violated and Gribble wrote to the authorities urging an inquiry but to no avail. Worse, the southern part of the reserve was handed over to two returned servicemen—Overheu and Hay—for settlement. They had already lost their licences to hire Aborigines because of excessive cruelty, and the course of the next few years was set. Further murders and violence followed over the next four years, culminating in Australia's second-last large-scale massacre of Aborigines just a few months after James' ordination.

In May 1926 there was a confrontation between Aborigines and the settlers.[58] Hay confronted an elder, Lumbulumbia, flogged him and broke his spears. The old man then killed Hay with a broken spear. Retaliation was brutal and disproportionate. Wyndham police organised a party of thirteen who rode through the area, "capturing, chaining and finally killing every Aborigine they could find."[59]

Gribble had initially assisted the police, believing that the authorities had the right to arrest and bring Hay's killer to justice but also wanting to find out for himself what they were doing and preventing at least one massacre. Once he got the police off the reserve via the mission's launch boat, he despatched James Noble, an expert tracker, to investigate.

Harris extracts this passage from the Forrest River Mission journal of 21 June 1926 that led to the subsequent Royal Commission:

> Noble returned this evening, having found
> the spot on the Upper Forrest where the
> police shot and burned their native prisoners.
> He brought back a parcel of charred remains.
> The natives were shot on stones in the bed of
> the river. Blood is still all around.[60]

At least thirty of those killed were known to the missionaries. Local Aborigines claim that there were hundreds of victims; the men were shot, and women and children were clubbed to death in several locations. The exact figure will never be known as investigations were delayed by the unwillingness of the government, church, politicians and locals in Wyndham to heed Gribble's pleas for an immediate investigation.

Commissioner Woods only began his work in 1927, with most of the evidence having been washed away by the wet season of 1926. Still, twelve victims were able to be identified. The Wyndham police were found to have acted in self-defence and were transferred out of the region. The entire white Wyndham community shunned Gribble and the mission, which therefore began to struggle to operate. Gribble was to leave soon after, in 1928, sacked by the ABM, and with the local Aboriginal people weeping at his departure. The Nobles followed in 1932.[61]

Rev Ernest Gribble enabled the ministry of James and Angelina Noble. He was a complex man whose legacy in missions is contested.

1933

Epilogue and conclusion

Gribble moved back to Queensland to serve at Palm Island. He wrote to ask the Nobles to join him there, but for unknown reasons they were not allowed to reside on the island. Instead they lived on nearby Esk Island and ministered across both. James' health was failing and within a year the family relocated back to Yarrabah; James had indicated he wanted to die at home.

The picture of James' final years at Yarrabah is of an Aboriginal man returning to his cultural roots and loves: fishing, hunting, teaching younger men how to make shields, boomerangs, stone tomahawks, and spear tips from stingray spines. He maintained Christian ministry in visiting the sick and leading services but was also growing senile.[62] James Noble died in a Cairns hospital on 25 November 1941 and is buried at Yarrabah.

Angelina was the "old lady," a term of respect and honour; the one who administered discipline to the younger children, the matriarch of the Noble clan. She outlived James by twenty-three years, dying at Yarrabah on 19 October 1964. She is buried with

NATIVE CLERGYMAN DEAD

TOWNSVILLE, Wednesday. — The Rev. James Noble, an aboriginal clergyman, died in the hospital in Cairns last night. For the last 40 years he had been a leader in mission work among his own people, and had attained deacon's orders in 1925. He had taken an important part in the journeys and missionary ventures of the Rev. E. R. B. Gribble, and enjoyed the high esteem of his people. For the last few years, in declining health, he had lived at his old home at Yarrabah.

The Courier-Mail,
Thursday 27 November 1941

him. Her life and ministry are remembered and honoured today in the Angelina Noble Centre.[63]

Gribble was a complex man and his legacy in missions is contested. However, his policy of seeking to empower Aboriginal people enabled the ministry of James and Angelina Noble. They followed their mentor in their willingness to leave their home culture, live among the people they sought to serve, learn new languages and practices, teach and preach the gospel of Christ, give their people practical help and vocational skills, and love and build up the church wherever they lived.

As missionaries, James and Angelina played a part in the founding of Kowanyama and Ngukurr, the Mitchell and Roper River Missions. Remembering with fondness that black people brought them the gospel is part of the Ngukurr story, a theme later mirrored in Ugandan bishop Festo Kivengere's brief tour of the region in 1959. A Gunbalanya Aboriginal man reflected on Festo's ministry with words that would have applied just as well to James Noble:

> We are so glad that our brother in Christ
> has come here. He speaks of the same Jesus
> we know, he speaks of the sure love of God
> which we know. He tells us those things
> which the [white] missionaries have told us
> for years, but now we can see clearly that
> Jesus Christ is also the Saviour of black men.[64]

James and Angelina's ministry at Forrest River gave the Christians of the nation hope that something positive might be done for the dispossessed Aboriginal people of the land. That dream was shattered, and too little is known of what later happened to those who had become Christians at the mission and survived the atrocities of that time.

The Nobles are still remembered and honoured at Yarrabah, which remains a centre of Aboriginal Christian life in Australia's north. Bishop Arthur Malcolm—the first Aboriginal Anglican Bishop, consecrated in 1985—was a descendant who acknowledged his debt to James for paving the way.[65] His successor, Jim Leftwich, was another descendant. The Nobles' legacy is ongoing.

What are some important themes emerging from the James and Angelina Noble story?

Their story reminds us that colonisation brought much suffering and evil to the First Peoples of Australia but also that Christians acted to save and protect, and indeed achieved that purpose. We must remember Barnabas Roberts' words: "I thank God for the missionaries. If the missionaries had not come, we would all be dead."[66] That is not to say that missionaries got everything right or that the following history is faultless—far from it. But in an age when all things Christian or missionary are too easily dismissed as "colonialist" or "patriarchal" or "culture-destroying," their story demands a more nuanced and fairer assessment.

Angelina's contribution to James' success as the first ordained Aboriginal Anglican must not be underestimated. Her gender and her own story of trauma led women to trust in her, James and other missionaries. Her practical and teaching skills were frequently noted. But above all, it was her giftedness in languages that made the communication of the Christian message so effective. As Lamin Sanneh has shown, people are much more effectively evangelised and discipled in their heart language. The God of the Bible is brought close to them and is not a foreign god—rather, he speaks our own tongue.[67] The effectiveness of James's preaching ministry stood on the shoulders of Angelina's work as a faithful interpreter. They were a remarkable gospel team.

Along with Angelina's language learning would have come an understanding and appreciation of each culture she and James were immersed in. Our contemporary expertise in what it takes to be truly effective in cross-cultural Christian ministry leads us to the inescapable conclusion that without Angelina, James would have been just another well-meaning but ultimately ineffective missionary. Angelina's story is as important as James' and together they were used mightily by God.

Both Angelina and James' stories of individual and combined suffering remind us of the words of Jesus Christ: "Take up your cross and follow me;"[68]

"Unless a grain of wheat falls into the earth and dies, it remains just a single grain; but if it dies, it bears much fruit."[69] They understood and lived the Christian life of suffering first, glory later. They understood their identity as servants of others for the sake of Christ. Although preyed upon by others, they did not see themselves as victims. Saved by Christ to serve, they led redeemed lives of sacrificial service to others—especially the most vulnerable and marginalised of their fellow First Peoples.

Perhaps most arresting of all is the fact that their missionary heart was for those other First Peoples of Australia. We recall the mentoring and encouragement they received from the missionaries Boyce and Gribble. How significant these must have been! For James and Angelina did not stay in the North Queensland of their birth, but ventured further afield to serve those in Arnhem Land and North West Australia. They looked beyond their own and known people and places to other black people who needed Jesus Christ; from Jerusalem to Judea and Samaria, and to the ends of the earth.[70] Their courage in the face of the dangers, uncertainties and guaranteed deprivations of those adventures continues to inspire us today.

At the centenary of James' ordination, we recall the Angelina and James Noble story. We remember their faith and courage, activism and leadership. We believe James' words: "I speak for black people." We determine to follow where Angelina and James have led in finding hope in the faith and love of Christ.

> You then, my child, be strong in the grace
> that is in Christ Jesus; and what you have
> heard from me through many witnesses
> entrust to faithful people who will be able
> to teach others as well. Share in suffering
> like a good soldier of Christ Jesus.

Paul to Timothy,
2 Timothy 2:1–3, NRSVA

Angelina Noble (left), Rev James Noble and
their family at the Forrest River Mission,
where the three youngest children were born.
1925

Mr James Noble
Report to the Ninth
Australian Church Congress
May 1925

I am very lone. I am the only black people left.
When I speak like this you know what I mean.
I wish we could come back two or three hundred
years ago, and there were plenty of blacks, and we
might have saved them, but it is now too late. It is
not your fault; but they tried to live like you, so
they died. The only way to save their life is Christian grace and teaching. They must learn to look
after themselves; to live clean and to take care of
themselves; all this is to be done because you are
trying to save their life. When I was in Melbourne
someone said, "Leave the black people alone."
Why didn't they say that long ago, when they were
all over the country? Another thought is, let black
people rule over themselves. Too late, now! Only a
few! I hope they can rule over themselves and I can
say thank you. They are thankful now, especially to
the Government who gave land, and at the Forrest

River, where I am. They want more—to run about in, in the bush. The Government is good, the Government does its best, and the Church does, too. But we want more Churches in the Forrest River. Only one Church there, and more black people than in any part of Australia. Only a few where the Mission are. Three Missions—Church of England, Presbyterian and Roman Mission—keep black people alive. People drifting into other places; two more Christian Missions and we could save black people in that country. Alone they will die out because they have no country of their own. They have no black people to stand and speak for them when I die. I can speak for those black people because you have been kind to them and given them a good home. A mission is not an easy thing to start; very hard to start. They teach the same time and they work; teaching those black people to lead a new life. They lead black people to the best way to live they want to live like them. A missionary is a great picture to black people; the way he lives; the character he has; and always ready to face hardship. By loving him the missionary teaches people to love God, too. Black people change lives very quick. God answers prayer very soon, as missionaries pray for them; that is how missionaries win. Black people begin to sing to the same God and love the same God. Only for the missionaries it's not very easy work. Missionaries' life very hard. Not good food to eat. At my good breakfast this morning with big bishops and men, I thought of missionary at home with only cup of tea sometimes. They show these black people how to live and love God. God will do it, not in missionaries' time, but in His own time. I know you will never forget to pray for those black people and missionaries, and so I am glad to stand before you, and am thankful to you.[71]

Painting in St Matthew's Church,
Ngukurr, tells the story of the arrival
of missionaries, bringing God's word,
resulting in a peaceful community.
1998

Bibliography

Paul A. Barker, Bradly S. Billings (eds), *Making the Word of God Fully Known: Essays on Church, Culture, and Mission in Honor of Archbishop Philip Freier.* Wipf and Stock: Eugene, Oregon, 2020.

Peter Berthon, Majorie Hall, William Hall, John Harris, Andrew Robertson, Carol Robertson (eds), *We Are Aboriginal: Our 100 years: from Arnhem Land's First Mission to Ngukurr Today.* St Matthew's Anglican Church: Ngukurr, 2008.

Kenneth Cable, Noel Pollard, Leonie Cable, *The Cable Clerical Index of clergy who served in the Anglican Church of Australia from 26 January 1788 through to those ordained or serving by 31 December 1961.* Unpublished MS. The *Cable Clerical Index* is a national treasure with a wealth of information in over 6570 entries. It was assembled by Ken and Leonie Cable and Noel Pollard over a number of decades. The card index is in the Moore College library; a version is available online at http://anglicanhistory.org/aus/cci/index.pdf last accessed 1 July 2025.

Philip L. Freier, *Living with the Munpitch: The History of Mitchell River Mission, 1905–1967.* PhD thesis, James Cook University, 1999.

H. T. Goss, *The Australian Blacks: The Appeal from the Never Never,* Church Missionary Association: Melbourne, 1909.

Ernest Gribble, *A Despised Race: The Vanishing Aboriginals of Australia.* Australian Board of Missions: Sydney, 1933.

Ernest Gribble, *Forty Years with the Aborigines.* Angus & Robertson: Sydney, 1930.

Ernest Gribble, *The Problem of the Australian Aboriginal.* Angus & Robertson: Sydney, 1932.

John Harris, *One Blood: 200 Years of Aboriginal Encounter with Christianity: A Story of Hope.* (2nd edition) Albatross: Sydney, 1994.

Geoff Higgins, *James Noble of Yarrabah.* Mission Publications of Australia: Lawson, NSW, 1981.

Wei-Han Kuan, *Foundations of Anglican Evangelicalism in Victoria: Four Elements for Continuity 1847–1937.* Wipf and Stock, Eugene, Oregon 2019.

Clive Morton, *Arthur Malcolm AO: Australia's First Indigenous Bishop.* Harry Edwin Clive Morton: Brisbane, 2005.

George Sombe Mukuka, *Call Me a Black Man, For That Is What I Am: Missionary Activity in Australia 1820–1990: James Noble and the "Aboriginalization" of the Australian Clergy*, PublishAmerica: Baltimore, 2013.

Lamin Sanneh, *Translating the Message: The Missionary Impact on Culture.* Orbis Books: Maryknoll, New York, 1989.

Murray Seiffert, *Gumbuli of Ngukurr.* Acorn Press: Melbourne, 2011.

Murray Seiffert, *Refuge on the Roper: The Origins of the Roper River Mission Ngukurr.* Acorn Press: Melbourne, 2008.

Lance Shilton, *Speaking Out: A Life in Urban Mission.* Centre for the Study of Australian Christianity: Sydney, 1997.

The Church and the New Age: Official Report of the Ninth Australian Church Congress, Held at Melbourne, 3rd to 13th May, 1925. The Congress Committee, Diocesan Registry: Melbourne, 1925.

George Tuthill Wood, *Report of Royal Commission of Inquiry into Alleged Killing and Burning of Bodies of Aborigines in East Kimberley and into Police Methods when Effecting Arrests.* Perth, 1927.

Notes

1 Higgins, *James Noble of Yarrabah*, 46–47.

2 Freier, *Living with the Munpitch: The History of Mitchell River Mission, 1905–1967*.

3 Jan Kociumbas, "Noble, James (1876–1941)," *Australian Dictionary of Biography* (ADB), National Centre of Biography, Australian National University, https://adb.anu.edu.au/biography/noble-james-7853/text13641, published first in hardcopy 1988, accessed online 11 July 2025.

4 Higgins, *James Noble of Yarrabah*. This volume was self-published and is now almost impossible to access, with only six library copies in Australia. Higgins interviewed descendants and family members who were firsthand eyewitnesses, recording in detail recollections that are nowhere else to be found.

5 Higgins, *James Noble of Yarrabah*, 1.

6 Gribble, *The Problem of the Australian Aboriginal*, frontispiece.

7 James' birth year is ascertained from the information supplied at his subsequent baptism and from the wedding register at Yarrabah.

8 Higgins, *James Noble of Yarrabah*, 1–5.

9 Higgins, *James Noble of Yarrabah*, 3.

10 "'Hoblah Jim.' First Native Clergyman. Rev. James Noble and his mentor." *The Daily News*, Thursday 17 September 1925, Perth, WA, 1882–1950, 7.

11 Mukuka, *Call Me a Black Man*.

12 *Cable Clerical Index*, 766.

13 "Hoblah Jim," 7.

14 Harris, *One Blood*, 518.

15 "Barlow, Christopher George (1858–1915)," ADB entry: https://adb.anu.edu.au/biography/barlow-christopher-george-5133, published first in hardcopy 1979, accessed online 11 July 2025.

16 Higgins wrongly dates Noble's arrival to "about 1896," which is too soon as the reason for Noble's move was Canon Edwards' death in early 1898.

17 Jan Kociumbas claims that Angelina was part-Aboriginal in this ADB entry: https://adb.anu.edu.au/biography/noble-angelina-8533/text13641, published first in hardcopy 1988, accessed online 11 July 2025. "James Noble," *Recorder*, Port Pirie, SA, 1919–1954, Thursday 26 March 1925, 3, mentions in passing that James was married to "Angelina, a half-caste." Higgins, who had access to family members at Yarrabah, makes no mention of this and remarks that she was born near Winton: *James Noble of Yarrabah*, 16.

18 Higgins, *James Noble of Yarrabah*, 16.

19 Photograph is at Higgins, *James Noble of Yarrabah*, 18. See also Register of Baptisms, Yarrabah Bellenden Kerr Aboriginal Mission, 1891–1927, AIATSIS MS3234. Transcript available online at http://www.cifhs.com/qldrecords/locyarrabah.html Last accessed 1 July 2019. Records show that an "Angelina" was baptised at Yarrabah in July 1902: unknown parents, no family name, age presumed as "about 21 years old." It seems reasonable to assume that this is Angelina Noble's record and that she would have arrived in Yarrabah earlier that year. If this is correct then Angelina was either a very young-looking twenty-one year old or her probable age was revised upward, probably to endorse her capacity to enter into marriage.

20 The Register of Baptisms indicates that: she was born around 1880; the date of her baptism was 24 May 1900; married to "Jimmie Noble;" and records her death in April 1902.

21 There are good reasons for giving priority to the contemporary written records. They are less likely to have been clouded by the passage of time; and there are no obvious social or political reasons for the records to have been amended or falsified at the time.

22 Higgins, *James Noble of Yarrabah*, 15, identifies the child as James Hilton, an identification followed by subsequent writers. This does not agree with the Register of Baptisms which identifies the child as Blanche Margaret; James Hilton is identified in the Register as the first child of Angelina and James. Higgins also describes Maggie as passing away a short time after her baby's birth.

23 See handwritten notes appended to the Register of Baptisms: "… zie Moore confirmed in Brisbane, died sunday 20. 7.1902."

24 See Yarrabah Marriages, 1901–1916, a transcript of a photocopy of a Register of Marriages, 1901–1916 (original lost) http://www.cifhs.com/qldrecords/YarrabahMarriages1901_1916.html, last accessed 1 July 2019.

25 See John Gribble's ADB entry at https://adb.anu.edu.au/biography/gribble-john-brown-3668/text5727, published first in hardcopy 1972, accessed online 11 July 2025.

26 John Harris provides an excellent overview of Gribble's ministry. See Harris, *One Blood*, 407–427.

27 Harris, *One Blood*, 502–503.

28 Gribble, *Forty Years with the Aborigines*, 117–118.

29 Gribble, *Forty Years with the Aborigines*, 122.

30 Higgins, *James Noble of Yarrabah*, ch 2. Also Harris, *One Blood*, 506.

31 Freier, *Living with the Munpitch*, 106. See chapter 4 for an account of the various expeditions that relate to the founding of the Mitchell River Mission, Kowanyama.

32 Freier, *Living with the Munpitch*, 133–134.

33 Freier, *Living with the Munpitch*, 133. See also Gribble, *A Despised Race*, 63.

34 Seiffert, *Refuge on the Roper*, ch 3.

35 Harris, *One Blood*, 696.

36 Harris, *One Blood*, 693–703. Also Berthon et al. (eds),
    We Are Aboriginal.

37 Despite the CMA being headquartered at St Paul's Cathedral
    in Melbourne, Huthnance was deaconed by the evangelical
    Bishop of Bendigo, John Langley, in January 1908, Joynt
    was also later deaconed by Langley in September 1918 for
    Carpentaria and the work at Roper River. See *Cable Clerical
    Index.* Then Archbishop of Melbourne, Henry Lowther
    Clarke was known to be antagonistic towards evangelicals
    and their endeavours centred around the CMA and Ridley
    College, and remained aloof. Wei-Han Kuan, *Foundations
    of Anglican Evangelicalism in Victoria: Four Elements for
    Continuity 1847–1937.* Wipf and Stock: Eugene, Oregon 2019.

38 Seiffert, *Gumbuli of Ngukurr*, 79.

39 Higgins, *James Noble of Yarrabah*, 19, contains this anecdote
    but with a slightly different form of words than a report
    of the incident in "James Noble," *Recorder*, Port Pirie, SA,
    1919–1954, Thursday 26 March 1925, 3.

40 Higgins, *James Noble of Yarrabah*, 19–20, from Yarrabah's
    Aboriginal News, 21 August 1908.

41 Harris, *One Blood*, 704.

42 Harris, *One Blood*, 705. Spelling updated to Kriol.

43 Harris, *One Blood*, 707. Seiffert, *Gumbuli of Ngukurr*, 79.

44 Higgins, *James Noble of Yarrabah*, 26.

45 *ABM Review*, June 1914. Extracted at Higgins, *James Noble
    of Yarrabah*, 26–31.

46 Higgins, *James Noble of Yarrabah*, 41–42.

47 Higgins, *James Noble of Yarrabah*, 39–45.

48 Gribble, *Forty Years with the Aborigines*, 180.

49 "Abo. Ordained" *The News*, Hobart, Tasmania, 1924–1925,
    Wednesday 16 September 1925, 4.

50 See "James Noble's Visit to Narrogin." *Great Southern Leader*, Pingelly, WA, 1907–1934, Friday 20 February 1925, 5. Searching for "James Noble missionary" on https://trove.nla. gov.au results in many newspaper reports of the tour from the various locations across that year. Last searched 1 July 2019.

51 "Missionary Exhibition," *South Western Times*, Bunbury, WA, 1917–1929, Tuesday 10 March 1925, 2.

52 "Brighton News," *Glenelg Guardian*, SA, 1914–1936, Thursday 18 June 1925, 4.

53 "Missionary Exhibition," *Newcastle Morning Herald and Miners' Advocate*, NSW, 1876–1954, Monday 29 June 1925, 5.

54 "Among the Blacks," *The Newcastle Sun*, NSW, 1918–1954, Monday 29 June 1925, 8.

55 Higgins, *James Noble of Yarrabah*, 46–47.

56 "Native Deacon: Tribesman in Holy Orders," *The Telegraph*, Brisbane, Queensland, Wednesday 16 September 1925, 3. The article noted that James had just completed a twelve-month tour of Australian cities and was now en route back to Forrest River. It also noted that, "Mr. Noble's success among the natives has been greatly aided by his wife Angelina, who speaks six native languages. They have six children." The eldest child, Ruth Roper, at age 18 was in charge of the mission school's dormitory.

57 "Ordination of James Noble," *ABM Review*, 12 November 1925, 139.

58 Higgins incorrectly dates these events to 1925 in *James Noble of Yarrabah*, ch 8.

59 Harris, *One Blood*, 512. See 511–514.

60 Harris, *One Blood*, 513.

61 The Forrest River Mission struggled on and was eventually closed in 1969. Aboriginal people were determined to resettle it as Oombulgurri in the early 1970s, receiving multiple injections of government assistance. It struggled

with dysfunction and abuse, closing in 2011. It seems that the blood of the slain cries out from the ground there.

62 Higgins, *James Noble of Yarrabah*, 61.

63 See https://angelinanoblecentre.com, last accessed 26 April 2025.

64 Lance Shilton, *Speaking Out: A Life in Urban Mission*. Centre for the Study of Australian Christianity: Sydney, 1997, 90. Shilton was one of the organisers of Kivengere's tour of the north, accompanied him, and took notes on the tour.

65 Higgins, *James Noble of Yarrabah*, foreword by Arthur Malcolm. See also Morton, *Arthur Malcolm AO*.

66 Harris, *One Blood*, 704.

67 Lamin Sanneh, *Translating the Message: The Missionary Impact on Culture*. Orbis Books: Maryknoll, New York, 1989. With thanks to David Williams for this reference and insight. Angelina's unsung contribution has been long recognised by Isabel Dale who suggested she be honoured by the naming of the Angelina Noble Centre: private email to the author from Evelyn Hibbert, 24 May 2019.

68 Matthew 16:24, NRSVA.

69 John 12:24–26, NRSVA.

70 Acts 1:8, NRSVA.

71 *The Church and the New Age: Official Report of the Ninth Australian Church Congress, Held at Melbourne, 3rd to 13th May, 1925*. The Congress Committee, Diocesan Registry: Melbourne, 1925, 328.

Photo credits

Acknowledgements

Thank you to Paul Barker who first invited me to write a chapter in the *Festschrift* for Archbishop Philip Freier. This book is based on that chapter. This would not have occurred without Philip's admiration for the Nobles and regular promotion of their story over the decades. The late Murray Seiffert was generous with resources and encouragement. Bronwyn Wood, archivist at the Australian Board of Missions, proves that hers is an invaluable and noble profession. Joy Sandefur kept insisting that the original chapter be published separately and made widely available—thank you for persisting!

Every author must take responsibility for all errors and opinions in their work. These would have been far more numerous and egregious without the eagle-eyed, wise and careful comments from Greg Anderson, David Williams, Chris Mulherin, Angela Chandler and Elspeth Collie. The book would have been far less focused and engaging without the skill, creativity and expertise of publisher Michael Collie.

We acknowledge that this book was researched and written on the lands of the Wurundjeri people and in heartfelt Christian fellowship with the people of Bagot, Ngukurr, Numbulwar, Urapunga, Minyerri and Angurugu. People known to me, living in places I have been privileged to visit in the Northern Territory, among whom I thank in particular:

Rosemary and Derek Snibson
Marjorie and William Hall
Stephanie and Joshua Mackenzie
Yulki Nunggumajbarr
Edwin Bundurr Rami
Rebecca and Samuel Gorfine